"I hope that every American, regardless of where he lives, will stop and about this and other related incidents. This nation was founded by backgrounds. It was founded on the principle that all men are created equal, and that the rights of every man are diminished when the rights of one man are threatened." - **Kennedy**

"Every great dream begins with a dreamer. Always remember, you have within you the strength, the patience, and the passion to reach for the stars to change the world."
- **Tubman**

"Four score and seven years ago our fathers brought forth on this continent, a new nation, conceived in Liberty, and dedicated to the proposition that all men are created equal."
- **Lincoln**

"Darkness cannot drive out darkness; only light can do that. Hate cannot drive out hate; only love can do that." - **King**

"Everything I do is for my people."
- **Sacagawea**

"We need to help students and parents cherish and preserve the ethnic and cultural diversity that nourishes and strengthens this community - and this nation."
- **Chavez**

"Women will only have true equality when men share with them the responsibility of bringing up the next generation."
- **Ginsburg**

"I am asking you to hold fast to that faith written into our founding documents; that idea whispered by slaves and abolitionists; that spirit sung by immigrants and homesteaders and those who marched for justice; that creed reaffirmed by those who planted flags from foreign battlefields to the surface of the moon; a creed at the core of every American whose story is not yet written: Yes, we can." - **Obama**

Dedicated to every child.
You are beautiful and worthy of love.
You are American.

Mommy, Am I American?

by Aila Malik

Illustrations by Dawood Marion

"Mommy, am I American?"

"Yes, Son. You were born on American land."

"Mommy, is Nasir American? He was born on Pakistani land."

"Yes. Nasir and his family became Americans when they promised to be a part of America and protect its values above any other place in the world."

"But Mommy, what are America's values?"

"Oh, my child! America is the land of dreams, where people are free to make their own choices about who they are and who they want to be. It is a place where Lady Liberty welcomes the world to show how accepting and strong our people are."

"America is a place where everyone – no matter the color of your skin, or who you love, what job you have, or who your mommy is – *everyone* is equally important. America reflects, and *believes* in, the spirit and the *voices* of its people."

The Boy shrugged his shoulders and said, "Oh, I thought Nasir was Muslim."

"Son, Nasir *is* Muslim and he is American."

"But Nasir has brown skin and his mommy dresses in clothes with too many colors."

"Yes, Nasir is brown-skinned and he is American. Nasir's mommy may wear different clothes, but what we wear and how we look doesn't make us more or less American."

"Mommy, what about Fernanda?

She said she came here when she was a baby."

"Fernanda has been in school with you for a very long time and her family works very hard for America. Even if people say that she is not an American on paper, she has an American spirit and America will protect her."

"I don't think so Mommy. America is going to build a wall so that Fernanda can't see her other family in Mexico."

"Yes, even the *idea* of a wall is sad, but walls cannot separate people's care and love for each other," said Mommy.

"But if you are sad about building walls, do you still love America?"

"I *love America* but I don't always like the choices that our leaders make. Just like I love you, but I don't always like your choices," said Mommy.

Mommy took a deep breath, and continued.

"We have to share our voice when we don't like a choice that American leaders are making. There are lots of people, like judges, activists, and community helpers, who can help keep America the land we love."

The Boy looked over at Mommy and saw her teary-eyed.

"Mommy, why are you crying," the boy asked.

"Son, I love the vision of America as a place where *everyone has a chance to* live a good life and be the best that they can be."

"So many people gave up so much to move America closer to that dream. You have learned about many of these people at school – our presidents like John F. Kennedy, Abraham Lincoln, and Barack Obama; and community leaders like Sacagawea, Harriet Tubman, Dr. Martin Luther King, Jr., Cesar Chavez, and Justice Ruth Bader Ginsburg – just to name a few..."

"...But so many more people that you will never know have done the same – like the original native people whose land was taken to build America and the brave men and women soldiers who fought for American values.

Sometimes my heart hurts for America, because it hurts for so many people who feel far away from that dream."

The Boy hugged Mommy. "I am hugging you from America," he said.

Mommy smiled and said, "What a beautiful thought!"

The Boy, hugged Mommy for a few minutes and then he asked, "Does America love me?"

Mommy thought about the question and replied, "When you stand up for American values – for the voice of all people – then you are showing your love for America."

"When you show you care for people who are different from you, you are loving America. When you show gratitude for what you have and kindness to those who have less than you, you are loving America..."

"...And when you say 'thank you' to people who give up spending time with their families to help our community and protect our freedom, then you are loving America."

Mommy took a deep breath and then she continued very slowly.

"When you show your love for America, you will feel her love in return."

Without saying a word, the Boy stood up, got a piece of paper and a pen, went to the dining table, and started writing.

Mommy walked over to the Boy and asked, "What are you doing?"

"I'm writing a note to Nasir and then I am going to write one for Fernanda."

"Oh really? What are you going to say?"

"I'm going to tell them I care about them and I want to learn more about their cultures ... I'm going to hug them from America."

Mommy smiled. "Son, that is *truly American.*"

The End

A Note from the Author

The day Donald Trump was elected as the 45th President of the Unites States of America, (November 2016), my husband and I had to console our sobbing and fearful 5th grader. He, along with his friends, had heard of remarks Trump had made about women, Muslims, and immigrants during the race. Just a few months later (January 2017), our son's fears were confirmed as Trump signed the Executive Order 13769, titled "Protecting the Nation from Foreign Terrorist Entry into the United States," or the "Muslim (travel) ban" and plans for the wall between Mexico and the US were being discussed.

I will never forget the day that this little boy earnestly asked me if he was in danger, though he was a US citizen. I realized that so many children who have mixed identities, suddenly found themselves in a world in which they felt insecure about "how American" they appeared to be.

As I prepared myself to engage in continued dialogue about America, my birthplace and the country I love, I held mixed emotions of my own disappointment and fear. I suddenly knew that being a strong and hopeful parent during this time, would take some authentic personal reflection and grace on my part.

I wrote this story through my own tears. It was my way of processing (and practicing) how I would define "patriotism" for my children. I ended up writing a love story to the American ideals of freedom and opportunity that so many people (directly and indirectly) sacrificed themselves for...and signing off with a hopeful plea for equity and community kindness.

Once this story took shape, I collaborated with my friend and amazingly talented colleague, Dawood Marion, who is like-minded in his hunger for inclusivity and justice. He brought this story to life with beautiful sepia-toned imagery, that invoked feelings of love, fear, sadness, hope, and nostalgia, all in the same series.

This book is NOT about partisan politics. It is about a joint vision of an equitable and inclusive America and an expression of gratitude to all those who have championed steps towards that end.

Facts About the American Heroes Referenced in this Book

"Everything I do is for my people."
Sacagawea (1788-1812)

A brave Shoshone Indian woman who, as interpreter, traveled thousands of wilderness miles with the Lewis and Clark Expedition (1804–06), from the Mandan-Hidatsa villages in the Dakotas to the Pacific Northwest. Her language, medicinal wisdom, and mothering of her infant during the journey were all critical factors that enabled the success of the expedition.

"Lewis & Clark at Three Forks", mural in lobby of Montana House of Representatives. Photograph: Edgar Samuel Paxson.

"Four score and seven years ago our fathers brought forth on this continent, a new nation, conceived in Liberty, and dedicated to the proposition that all men are created equal."
Abraham Lincoln (1809-1865)

The 16th president of the United States, Lincoln is often referred to by names like, Honest Abe, the Rail-Splitter, or the Great Emancipator. Now, ever-present to us on the $5 bill and penny, Lincoln is best known for preserving the Union during the American Civil War and ending slavery.

Public domain photograph by Alexander Gardner, Scottish photographer and war photographer.

"Every great dream begins with a dreamer. Always remember, you have within you the strength, the patience, and the passion to reach for the stars to change the world."

Harriet Tubman (1820-1913)

Born into slavery in Maryland, Harriet Tubman escaped to freedom in the North in 1849 to become the most famous "conductor" on the "Underground Railroad," or a network of people, African American as well as white, offering shelter and aid to escaped slaves. Tubman risked her life to lead hundreds of family members and other slaves from the plantation system to freedom. After the Civil War ended, Tubman dedicated her life to helping impoverished former slaves and the elderly. In honor of her life and by popular demand, the U.S. Treasury Department is expected to unveil a new $20 bill with her face, in 2028.

Portrait of Harriet Tubman, The Library of Congress from Washington, DC, United States.

"I hope that every American, regardless of where he lives, will stop and examine his conscience about this and other related incidents. This nation was founded by men of many nations and backgrounds. It was founded on the principle that all men are created equal, and that the rights of every man are diminished when the rights of one man are threatened."

John F. Kennedy (1917-1963)

JFK was the beloved 35th president of the USA. In his political career, he advocated for better working conditions, more public housing, higher wages, lower prices, cheaper rent, and more Social Security for the aged. Under his short presidency, JFK started the Peace Corps (a program where young Americans can volunteer for meaningful projects all over the world), worked on income tax cuts and civil rights measures (passed after his death), and committed the United States to put a man on the Moon by the end of the decade!

"We need to help students and parents cherish and preserve the ethnic and cultural diversity that nourishes and strengthens this community - and this nation."

Cesar Chavez (1927-1993)

Chavez was an American labor leader, community organizer, and Latino American civil rights activist who dedicated his life to improving the treatment, pay and working conditions for farmworkers. Along with Dolores Huerta, he co-founded the National Farm Workers Association (NFWA), which later merged to become the United Farm Workers (UFW) union. Cesar was willing to sacrifice his own life so that the union would continue and that violence was not used and fasted in protest on many occasions.

Library of Congress, Prints and Photographs Division, NYWT&S Collection, [LC-U9-32963- 20].

"Darkness cannot drive out darkness; only light can do that. Hate cannot drive out hate; only love can do that."

Dr. Martin Luther King, Jr. (1929-1968)

Martin Luther King Jr. was an American Christian minister and activist who became the most visible spokesperson and leader in the Civil Rights Movement from 1955 until his assassination in 1968. Dr. King won the Nobel Peace Prize in 1964, among several other honors. He continues to be remembered as one of the most influential and inspirational African-American leaders in history.

Library of Congress, Prints and Photographs Division, NYWT&S Collection, [CPH 3C26559].

"Women will only have true equality when men share with them the responsibility of bringing up the next generation."

Justice Ruth Bader Ginsburg (1933-)

Ruth Bader Ginsburg is an American lawyer and jurist who was the second female Associate Justice of the U.S. Supreme Court. As a lawyer, Justice Ginsburg passionately advocated for equality for women. Even at age 87, Justice Ginsburg is an active member of the Supreme Court. An icon of the new generation for her stances on equity, she has been affectionately named as the "Notorious RBG."

"I am asking you to hold fast to that faith written into our founding documents; that idea whispered by slaves and abolitionists; that spirit sung by immigrants and homesteaders and those who marched for justice; that creed reaffirmed by those who planted flags from foreign battlefields to the surface of the moon; a creed at the core of every American whose story is not yet written: Yes, we can."

Barack Obama (1961-)

Barack Obama was the two-term 44th president and the first African-American president of the United States. Obama advocated for health care for poor people and worked hard to bridge foreign diplomatic relations with countries to decrease tensions (i.e. a nuclear agreement in Iran, communications with Cuba, and withdrawal of troops from Iraq). Throughout his presidency, Obama struggled with increased partisanship in the House and Senate. In 2009, President Obama was awarded the Nobel Peace Prize for "extraordinary efforts to strengthen international diplomacy and cooperation between people".

About the Author Aila Malik

A lawyer by schooling and nonprofit executive by trade, Aila Malik has been a change-agent in her community and the nonprofit sector, at large, for over two decades. Aila earned her B.S. in Environmental Science from UC Santa Barbara, JD from Santa Clara Law School, and has received recognition for her leadership, activism, and tireless service. In 2015, Aila founded a unique management-consulting firm, Venture Leadership Consulting, partnering with not-for-profit organizations to drive performance and scale solutions that close systemic gaps of inequity.

Aila lives with intention as a compassionate advocate of community kindness, planet protection, and family togetherness. As a mother of three children, Aila is deeply committed to contributing to a world in which disparity does not limit people's access to opportunity.

Aila's other passion projects have been a children's book (published in 2013), focused on developing a child's coping skills in navigating the home-to-school transition, Pocket Mommy (visit AilaMalik.com for details), and her yearlong global journey with her family in 2018-19 which is still currently being documented FranklinStreetGlobetrotters.org.

About the Illustrator Dawood Marion

Dawood Marion, www.dawoodmarion.com, has a history of using art to express himself and empower others. Professionally, Dawood studied entertainment illustration at Gnomon School of Visual Effects in Hollywood. Since then, Dawood has worked as a conceptual and character design illustrator in film and video games, authored four books, created an instructional video series some of which can be found on his own YouTube channel (@DawoodMarion), and executed two documentary films. For over a decade he has shared his passion for art through teaching both drawing/painting, digital illustration and sculpture to youth and adults as well as in the juvenile hall system as a freelance artist and nonprofit practitioner.

Personally, Dawood's lived experience serves as his motivation to help others through art and his own example. Dawood's activism ranges from living lightly on the planet to fostering community kindness in the next generation as a father of his beautiful children. When interviewed about Mommy, Am I American? Dawood had this to say:

"There was a point, as a freelance artist collaborating on projects, that I struggled to find my voice through my work, while maintaining the importance of creating art and being an artist. This book is one of the most fulfilling projects I've worked on because it's timely and skillfully speaks to relevant issues in our society. This project was an agent of clarity for me while working on it and I believe it will prove valuable for youth as well as adults finding power and claiming their identity in America."

Our Role as #ParentActivists in #ParentingActivism for our Future Change-Champions

As a society, we are simmering in crisis. As we stand in a broth of tension and pain, resulting from years of environmental destruction and humanitarian abuse, we are reaching a boiling point. It is our responsibility to foster activism and awareness in the next generations to evaporate this messy mixture. It's time we stepped into our roles as #ParentActivists and begin #ParentingActivism in our future change-champions.

It's time to turn up the **HEAT! Humility-Empathy-Action-Togetherness**

Humility: A modest view of one's own importance.

Humility helps us create space to observe our surrounding environments because it removes the focus on ourselves. When we learn more about other people's stories, we often recognize our own privilege. *Examples: Go on a hike. Try new foods together. Listen to different genres of music and visit new neighborhoods. Meet new people and learn about their cultures.*

Empathy: The ability to understand and share the feelings of another.

The recognition of our own privilege motivates us to help others. We must model and instill a core value that we are all interconnected; our ability to care for others and our planet, in turn helps us to live a safer, healthier, and more fulfilled life. *Examples: Help your children understand their own "big feelings" and relate them to experiences in story characters when reading or watching movies together.*

Action: The act or process of doing something, typically to achieve an aim.

Support your child to "act" upon an interest area or cause. Remember the "humility" aspect of our activism should focus on our ability to "partner with" people and organizations, not "save" or "co-opt the autonomy or voices" of beneficiaries. *Examples: Help them raise funds for a charity through work they do. Teach them to have respect for community helpers. Help them amplify their own personal perspective on social justice issues through creative art projects.*

Togetherness: The state of being close to another person or other people.

Stay physically and emotionally close as a family and engage in regular "protected family time" and intentionally fun rituals together. Being and doing together in a consistently safe environment creates security and a sense of belonging. With that foundation, children are more likely to stay vulnerable, humble, and motivated to lean-in! *Examples: Let the kids plan family games. Sit in a room and read your own books in quiet togetherness for 20 minutes a day. Develop rituals for special days or milestones that are unique to your family.*

Get more tips and examples of ways you can turn up the HEAT at www.ailamalik.com
Icon made by Freepik from www.flaticon.com

Made in the USA
Monee, IL
12 July 2020